THE GAME OF LIFE

PRECIOUS JAMES

Unless otherwise indicated, Scripture quotations are from the New Living translation and the New King James Version of the Holy Bible.

ISBN: 9798846117570

DEDICATION

To Jesus, my inspiration
Thank you.

CONTENTS

EPISODE 1
THE GAME OF LIFE

And the city lieth foursquare, and the length is as large as the breadth: and he measured the city with the reed, twelve thousand furlongs. The length and the breadth and the height of it are equal. Rev 21:16

Come!!! I will show you "a city" equal in length, breadth, and height, this is the New Jerusalem. Remember you are "a city" set on a hill that cannot be hidden

Growing up I saw different shades of people in business, ministry, academics, career, etc.

•••

It was beautiful because it occurred to me that there were varieties in life to choose from. Along the line, I discovered something quite absurd; I observed some form of extremeness in most of these persons. This was quite disturbing and I became intrigued about the subject matter, extremeness. As fascinated as I was, I realized that some of these persons were consumed by this extreme nature that was in them. This made me see the dangers of being so extreme.

Extremeness simply means excess, too much, highest degree, far beyond the normal, which only keeps one at an edge. For instance, for some people, it's all about work, some church, others, one particular thing, like a routine throughout their life:

nothing new to add.

As a growing child looking for a landmark to follow, I imagined telling myself if these were all to life, it's definitely going to get boring sooner than I expected.

Many of us are aware of the core people; in our context, we call them *"co-co"* or *"holics."*

Janel was turning into that; she had been trying to grow her spiritual life which was so admirable. She loved God dearly, but along the line, she found herself not wanting to do anything else in life, she stopped schooling, started wearing her ' mother-sized' outfits, and stopped relating with people except with those who were somewhat like her. Later, she started detesting people and even condemned many others. Anyone who didn't appear like her was a sinner and was doomed for hell fire.

At some point she wasn't relating with the physical anymore, a physical Janel living in a physical world could only relate with the spiritual, she had gone extreme. Many years passed and after being faced with the hurdles of life, with little or no fruit in her life, she went astray, turned her back on all that she once believed, and even criticized it.

As I thought about this, even more, it dawned on me that Janel lacked a balanced knowledge of life as some of us are today. We are so energetic to play the game of life but if not properly understood just like Janel there are unintended consequences it can result to.

EPISODE 2
THE GAME OF LIFE

Life can be likened to a game played with dice. Dice is a labeled cube having six sides. In this context, the game of life will be elaborated with the *game of parchisi* commonly known as the *Ludo Game*. Ludo is a board game for two or four players, in which players race their tokens/pieces from start to finish according to the roll of a dice. Similarly, a dice with six sides is tossed in the game of life.

It's important to note that the first phase of the Ludo Game is to get a true dice, a true dice is so balanced with all six sides labeled, or else it would stand as a mere cube.

So also, is it with the game of life. Life is the tosser and you are the dice. As young people, life will toss you around, to and fro, and shake you hard, if you are not a true dice–balanced with labeled six sides, then you may be forced to quit the game.

Beautiful Janel had only one side to which she was extreme and when she was tossed. She lost the game. Just like in every game, in the game of life, there are rules. These I'll call Life Rule; these are very important as long as you are living.

The first rule is that "You must intentionally build your dice." Your dice have to be balanced and labeled with six sides.

It is not as easy as you think, but note that when life tosses you, good and bad things will surely happen to you. In life at some point of the toss, you will be frustrated, shattered, ridiculed, and abused. It is not a curse. It is just part of your training. But yet you will be so loved, appreciated, and celebrated, this is life, and to everything, there is a season.

So, therefore, you must make a cautious effort to have labeled six sides because all sides are very important in the game of life. For you to play the game of life and squeeze out all value from it, you must be intentional to build these six sides and they will include:

Spiritual Side: It is the most important because it controls every other aspect of life. You must understand that you are first, a spirit. You have a soul and live in a body, and you must seek God first and every other thing will be added or followed.

Social Side: We are physical beings connected in one way or the other. Our relationships are very important because it is a priceless currency and can buy what money cannot buy.

Educational side: The day you stop learning that day you start dying. Education is related to everything that requires you to learn, it may be a skill, academics, educative books, occupation, etc.

Financial Side: Relates to anything that fetches money, a source of income. It could come from a business, a profession, a career, talent or skill, etc.

Health Side: It is said that health is wealth, so true. We must make a conscious effort to watch what we eat, wear, and our surroundings.

Emotional Side: This has to do with your mind, a very powerful tool in this world. You are what you listen to and absorb. The people you surround yourself with and the information you take in can build or destroy you.

You must sit down and build yourself intentionally!! Work out your salvation. You can play this game of life with your friend, two, or four players just like the game of Ludo. Married couples can play the game of life with their spouse too. Intentionally play and build these six sides so that when you are tossed by life, you will come out as gold and be more than a conqueror. By that I mean, there should be a balance between the spiritual side, social side, educational side, financial side, health side, and emotional side.

The second rule in the game of life is that 'A side activates the game.' Let me make this very clear, in Ludo, for the game to start you need the highest side, 'a six precisely to begin.' This is the same with the game of life, yes you spend time building all sides, but there's a particular side that will be so prevalent. This is more like a side that you will be popularly known for, that is the highest side of you and, in most cases, that is what activates the game.

The third rule in the game of life is 'invest your tokens*(potentials)* on your sides.' Your tokens are your potential.

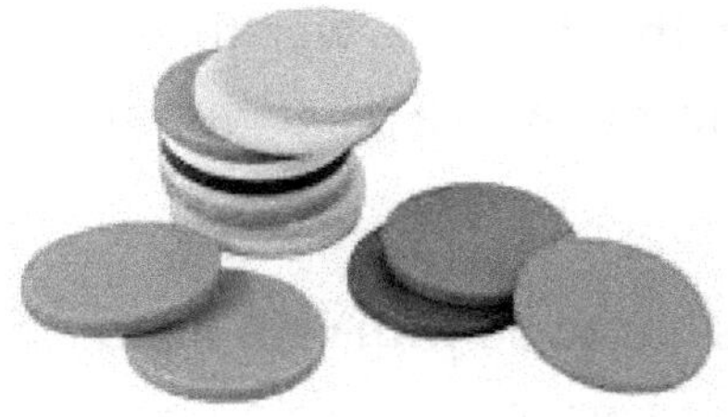

You must discover yourself, your potential, your abilities, and master your strengths. These are the tokens you would run with. You must sit down and discover this. In discovery, you must starve yourself of something that will distract you like movies, chatting, and things that are not adding to your life. You must be focused because it is a serious game. No more wasting your time on nonsense. Acquire value– value are things not tangible. Just like knowledge–difference between me and you are what I know. knowledge can be gotten from reading educative books (not romance novels), Bible, and listening to relevant audio and video tapes.

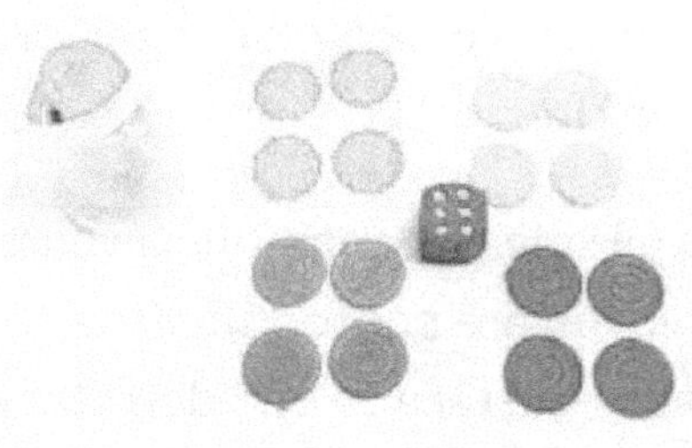

Invest in your social side by building your manners, learning basic etiquette in eating, talking, walking, etc. Also, build your self-esteem, there should be no more inferiority complex and jealousy. Furthermore, using the five magic words: sorry, thank you, please, forgive me, and pardon me, would enhance a better relationship with all around you.

Invest in your education by disciplining yourself to do well in whatsoever your hands find to do. If you are a singer, a baker, a hairdresser, or a teacher, always strive to be the best. Watch videos, read books, and google how to be the best in my field and work. Even if you don't arrive there, you will end up being so close. Aim to shoot the moon but even if you miss, you might end up hitting a star. Discover your purpose on earth and run with them

Invest in your health side by watching what you eat: your hygiene, your skin–the cosmetics we use, bleaching or not, exercise for a better physique, and improve your physical appearance. It is said that we are addressed the way we dress. It occurred to me that many young people hate being seen as good people. Therefore, they tend to dress inappropriately, but am glad to announce to you that it is good to be good, be the real you. Treasure your body, we admire celebrities looking forever young, we can look like that if we are conscious of it

Invest in your financial side by generating a source of income at any point in your life. You are not too small to start making money legally. This side makes the race sweet, don't let greed get over you and force you into doing the wrong thing. If you chose to be poor you are greedy, be rich and generous. Start making your own money now from a skill or talent and learn the act of saving and investing.

Invest in your emotional side by learning about the right mindset through books, audio, etc. Recondition your mind, be transformed by the renewal of the word, and learn how to control your emotions.

Invest in your spiritual side by reading your Bible, and praying every day if you want to grow, this is a secret to rise in the kingdom of God. Scriptures said 'and Elijah, a man of like passion with us, prayed earnestly that they shouldn't be rain and there was no rain'. The spiritual controls the physical, hence you must make a deliberate effort to build this side, get videos, get an audio bible, listen to them while you do daily activities, and let them saturate your head space.

Some salient aspect of life has been ignored, balancing all these, simply makes you mature, and you will be able to know how to handle some things in life. We are the leaders of tomorrow, and to lead tomorrow, we need to prepare now. Once you are investing your potential, you will be so focused and sometimes forget unproductive activities such as engaging in chi-chats.

Jesus was 12 years old, yet he had already started talking to elders and they listened Keenly. And here we are far older than us but we can't even talk to our mates and they listen. You are not a child anymore, invest in all your sides

The fourth rule in the game of life is ‘opposition must come.’ The game of life prepares you for life. In the Ludo Game, sometimes before coming out from your house, tokens are waiting to kill or stop you, sometimes they are in your house and sometimes some are piled up behind your house. The truth is that you will be opposed in life, be cautious of this, and remember challenges are for a while and each trial you will pass through will only make you stronger. And as it is in the Ludo Game, at times we manage to scale through and then we come to a place of safety.

The fifth rule in the game of life is that ‘you only have to get started.’ It is beautiful to be tossed by life, or else you are out of the game. While some persons try so hard in the Ludo Game to get a six (the side that announces them most), some persons get 2 six, 4 six, 6 six. They start the race and run with great speed. Fine, sometimes they win, but most times they end up not winning the game, perhaps because they lack other sides just like Janel did. This is to tell you in the game of life, patience is required and it is a virtue even as contentment is a great gain. The fact that you have not started does not mean it is the end, it is only a beginning for you to get started.

The sixth rule in the game of life is that ‘you don't always get what you want.’ The race is often not to be sweet. You will be disappointed, battered, and shattered. Sometimes you may be stretched to survive. Why? You may want to ask me. You need it, says life, you need it to become a better and stronger you. You need it to succeed after you have been tried you will come out as gold.

EPISODE 3
THE GAME OF LIFE

In the game of life, just like the Ludo Game. It is a bit of luck and skill. When life tosses you, whatsoever side that surfaces are by luck (by chance). But for your tokens/potentials to keep running, it is by skill, that you will be so intentional and make a cautious effort to succeed against all odds

You are a dice with six sides, and are they labeled or blank? Be a true dice, be so balanced and labeled with all six sides so when life tosses you, you will soar in the midst of it all and come out standing strong. Many of us indeed have these sides but some sides are suffering. I tell you this, be so balanced that when someone sees one side of your dice, they will think that is all about you because you will live it very well, and when they realize there is more to you (other sides), you will be a wonder to many (a living epistle-an example of the believers)

Playing the game of life is very important because it helps you Fastrack your life. Sometimes in reality when we fail in an aspect of this game, we think we are total failures but that is not true

For example, Boluwa fails in her academics, she has been so ridiculed, scorned, and cursed, while some say she's good for nothing, others have written her off completely and call her a dull girl who doesn't know anything. little did she realize that her academics is only an aspect of her life and do not determine her entire life

This game helps you see the very inside of yourself and strive for balance, are we all perfect? it depends on the yardstick you define the word perfect. But Almighty God says be thou perfect? meaning perfection is a possibility and then he calls a man named

"Job" perfect.
If God believes we can be perfect and calls us to perfection then I too believe God that we can be perfect.

The first time I played the game of life, I cried, My real-life result? So terrible? I have never gotten an "F" in my academics from childhood till date, but I got an F in an aspect of my life in the game, oh I cried and I repented and holy spirit helped me, I became more cautious and more intentional about my life and within the space of three months, I was amazed how my life changed, I rose in all aspect of my life and my results changed, my F and E's turned to A's and B's

I have played this game with lots of persons and have seen tremendous change over years, Few persons that had poor results improved, they began blasting A's, B's and C's

The Game of Life is played in the beginning of sections in life. It is a game of truth and circles on self-reflection and evaluation. The past is revealed and the future is planned for. The game of life is a call to balance and perfection, The game reviews your lapses, limitation, and how much of help you need from God. You will see your real Life result glaring, this is very serious and powerful game, it shows you your life at a glance, your real life score, and then for some you will see how much of you have wasted time, resources, talent, no accountability, no credibility and how much you have offended your maker, the one who sent you to earth. And sincerely and unashamedly you have to ask for forgiveness, cry for mercy and change, repent from your past ways. He will forgive you, correct you, comfort you and applaud you. He will make you an example of the believers, an epistle.

EPISODE 4

HOW TO PLAY THE GAME OF LIFE

The Game of Life is played in sections or seasons, quarterly, annually, etc. It can be played by one or more players, by family, friends, at church gatherings, or meetings, I personally play this game with my team, friends, and myself, I cautiously do this something to make people think about their life, Truth is that we have become so busy that we don't have time to plan and think of our life, this game is a guide to number our days so we can apply our hearts to wisdom

Get a notebook and pen as we are about to play the game of Life, This game is your life on paper, yes it important than your exams, if you fail in this game you have truly failed in life, although there is a solution as long as one is alive there is always a solution and hope.

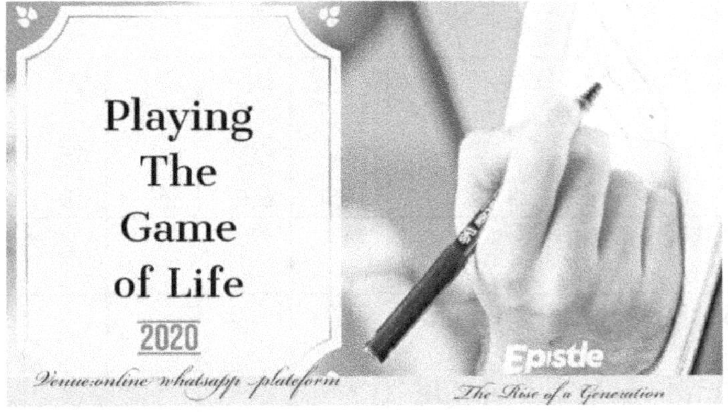

STEP 1
Reflect and review your previous section

This is a moment of intense reflection, think about your life so far, especially for the section you are reviewing. How has your life been, imagine the parable of the talent, how the master went away for a while and at his arrival he ask, how far, tell me how you have utilized this season, how you used your talent, and what profits did you make to yourself, society and the kingdom come. And sincerely spell it out in the book you are with, so get one if you are yet to

There's no need to lie, he knows the truth, just for once be sincere to yourself and God
You will be rating yourself on each side on a scale of 1-100 for every side.

So let's begin

THE GAME OF LIFE (Self Evaluation Form)							
NAME: DATE:		SECTION OF REVIEW:					
	Six Sides of a Dice	A 70-100	B 60-69	C 50-59	D 45-49	E 40-44	F 0-39
1.	**Spiritual Side**						
2.	**Social/Relationship Side**						
3.	**Emotional/Mental Side**						
4.	**Educational Side**						

5.	**Health Side**						
6.	**Finance Side**						

1. Spiritual Side
Moments of Self Reflection

1. How is my spiritual life?
2. What effort have I contributed to building my spiritual life in this past section?
3. How is my service in the house of God?
4. Did I engage in spiritual activities like Prayer, word, and fellowshipping with spirit to grow my spiritual life?
5. Is my life Revealing/ Glorifying God and contributing to the kingdom mandate "Thy kingdom come"?

On a scale of 1-100 Please rate your spiritual side

2. Social/Relationship Side
Moment of self-reflection

1. How has my social life been in this section?
2. Was I intentionally building quality relationships in this section?
3. Was I friendly and approachable or I am always grumpy and a snub?
4. How did I want my social life to look like (classic, mild, Exquisite, etc.)? Did I achieve what I want for myself?

On a scale of 1-100 Please rate your social side

3. Educational side

This is one of the broadest sides, it involves anything that requires your adding knowledge, learning new things, and adding value It can be broken into the following subset

1. Academics
2. Business/Work
3. Assignment/Purpose

In the game of life, each is reviewed depending on the categories an individual fall under. From the game, you realize that your academics although important don't define you

I. Academics

Moments of Self Reflection

1. How has my academic performance been?
2. What effort did I contribute to have good grades?
3. Was I too busy and distracted and pay little or no attention to my academics?
4. Did I engage in activities like studying hard, getting materials, solving past questions, attending classes, etc. to build my academics?

II. Business/Work

Moments of Self Reflection

1. How is business/work?
2. Was I diligent in my business/work?
3. Did I do well with whatever my hand finds to do?
4. Did I improve my business?
5. What effort did I contribute to building my business/work?
6. How have my service to my clients/customers and organization been?
7. Did I enlighten myself in these areas?

II. Assignment/Purpose

Moments of Self Reflection

1. Have I discovered purpose yet?
2. How do I discover purpose?
3. What cautious effort did I put to achieve my purpose or assignment this year
4. Is my assignment/purpose Revealing/ Glorifying God and contributing to the kingdom mandate "Thy kingdom come"?

Having done all, on a scale of 1-100 Please rate your Educational side

4. Financial Side

Moments of Self Reflection

1. How has my financial life been?
2. Why am I poor financially?
3. What knowledge do I have about financial education?
4. Can I give an account of how I used all the money I got this season?
5. What did I do about savings and investment?
6. Did I engage in kingdom laws of wealth, tithing offering, etc.?
7. Did I get consistent cash flow that will make me retire early in life?
8. What books and investments did I engage in?
9. What aspect of my finances did I ignore?
10. Did I spend unnecessarily and was I accountable?

11. Did I change and form lasting financial habits?
12. What effort did I contribute to building my finance in this past section?

On a scale of 1-100 Please rate your financial side

5. Health Side

Countless stories of businessmen too busy to take care of their health have died due to stress or one sickness or the order because they paid little or no attention to these sides

Moments of Self Reflection

1. How much did I take care of myself in this section?
2. Did I eat a balanced meal or I was eating junk and anything anyhow?
3. Did I take care of my hygiene, cosmetics, deodorants, toothpaste, etc.?
4. How is my physical appearance- Did I were neat and ironed cloth or not?
5. Did I engage in exercise to keep fit?
6. Did I go for checkups when needful?
7. Did I improve my health?
8. Did I engage in scriptural prescription for good health and long life?
9. Did I get adequate knowledge I need for my health from books, audio, and seminars?

On a scale of 1-100 Please rate your health side

6. Emotional/Mental Side

Moments of Self Reflection

1. Do I have a positive mindset?

2. What did I learn about mindset and building Emotions?
3. Did I improve my mindset?
4. Did I engage biblical principles about mindset?
5. Did I leverage on books, audios and seminars to recondition my mind?

On a scale of 1-100 Please rate your mental side.

With the grading in the picture below assign A-F to your grades

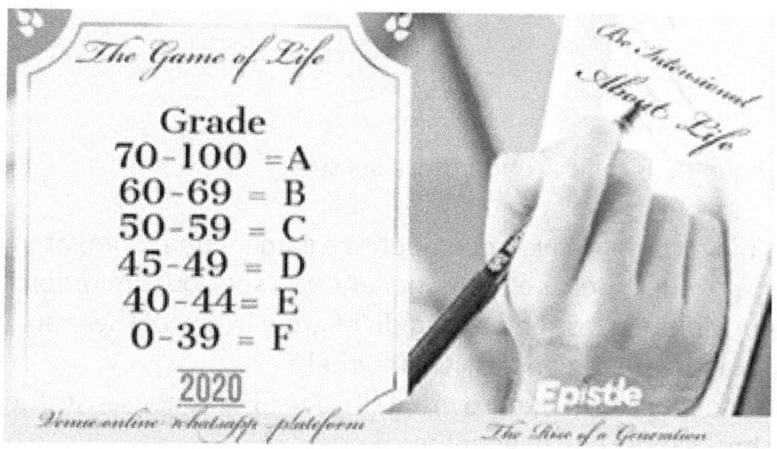

Your final result should look like this, this is your result, this is The Game Of Life

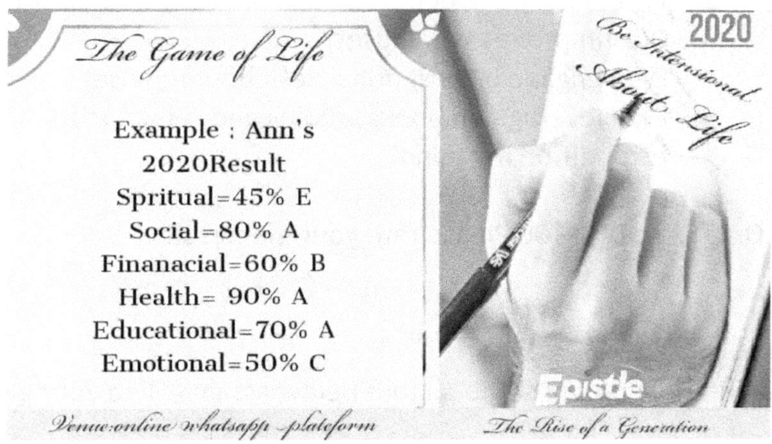

Our whole life is built around these six sides.

This is not a comparative or competitive game, but a moment of truth, self-reflection, and evaluation. As you see your limitation. Ask yourself the questions, why didn't I grow in any of these six areas, state them out and ask God for help.
We have defaulted in our growth, tell yourself this nonsense and childishness must end in your life.

THE GAME OF LIFE (SELF REFLECTION AND EVALUATION)				
NAME: **REVIEW:**		**SECTION OF DATE:**		
	Six Sides of a Dice	Poor	Average	Good
1.	**Spiritual Side**			
	How is my spiritual life? What effort have I contributed to building my spiritual life in this past section? Did I engage in spiritual activities like Prayer, word, and fellowshipping in the spirit to grow my spiritual life? Is my life Revealing/ Glorifying God and contributing to the kingdom mandate "Thy kingdom come"? How is my service in the house of God?			
2.	**Social/Relationship Side**			

	How has my social life been in his section? Did I intentionally build quality relationships in this section? I am friendly and approachable or I am always grumpy and a snub? What do I want my social life to look like (classic, Mild, Exquisite, etc.)? Have I found out what the word says about relationships? Did I build quality relationships? Do I read books and audio on relationships and friendship? If I fall into trouble are there at least three persons that can come for financial rescue			
3.	**Emotional/Mental Side**			

	Do I have a positive mindset? As a man thinketh so is he, could it be that the reason I am the way I am now is because of my mindset? What do I know about mindset and building emotions?			
4.	**Educational Side**			
	1. Academics How has my academic performance been? What must be done to improve in these areas? What is God's word concerning my education? How can I improve my academics, business, and assignment?			
	2. Business/Work Have I been diligent in my business? Do I do well with whatever			

	my hand finds to do?			
	3. Assignment/Purpose Have I discovered purpose yet? How do I discover purpose? What cautious effort did I put to achieve my purpose or assignment this year?			
5.	**Health Side**			
	How much do I take care of myself? Am I eating a balanced meal or eating junk and anything anyhow? I am taking care of my hygiene, cosmetics, deodorants, toothpaste, etc. How is my physical appearance- Do I wear ironed cloth or not? Do I engage in exercise to keep fit? Do I go for checkups when			

	needful? How much do I pay attention to improving my health? Do I take drugs, alcohol, and smoke that are detrimental to my health?			
6.	**Finance Side**			
	Why don't I have Money? What knowledge do I have about financial education? Can I give an account of how I used all the money got this season? What do I know about savings and investment? Do I engage in kingdom laws of wealth, tithing offering, etc.?			

STEP 2
PLAN FOR THE NEXT SECTION

Planning is the process of thinking through the activities required to achieve a desired goal. It is based on foresight it is much more detailed. Plan with God by setting clear S.M.A.R.T goals in the six areas. The acronym S.M.A.R.T signifies Specific, Measurable, Accurate, Realistic, and Time-bound.

Example: I will study one chapter every day of the book of proverbs in June.

In your book, write out your plan for the next section, what is the way forward, and how can you make it better, ask yourself the following questions below for each side and plan.

1. Spiritual Side

What is the way forward?

1. How do I develop my spiritual life? (List them)
2. What books, messages, and seminars can help me build my spiritual life? (List them)
3. What does God's word say about becoming spiritual? (List them)
4. What Activities should I do that can help build my spiritual life? (List them)

2. Social/Relationship Side

What is the way forward?

1. How do I build quality relationships? (state it)
2. What does the word of God say about relationships? (List them)
3. Where do I meet quality people and how do I approach them? (List them)
4. What books and audio do I need to listen to? (List them
5. What three persons do I want to consciously build quality relationships with? (List them)

3. Emotional/Mental Side
What is the way forward?

1. How do I improve my mindset? (List them)
2. What does God's word say about mindset? (List them)
3. What books, audios, and seminars can improve my mental/emotional life? (List them)
4. What do I do to develop my mind? (List them)

4. Educational Side

I. Academics
What is the way forward?

1. How do I improve on my Academics? (List them)
2. Are there books, audios, and seminars that can help improve my academic performance? (List them)
3. What does God's word say about my education? (List them)
4. What Activities should I do that can help build the Academics side? (List them)

II. Business/Work
What is the way forward?

1. How do I improve in my Business/work? (List them)
2. What books, audios, and seminars can help build my Business/work ethics? (List them)

3. What does God's word say about work and business? (List them)
4. What Activities should I do that can help build my business/work? (List them)

III. Assignment/Purpose

What is the way forward?

1. How do I improve in my fulfilling my assignment and purpose on earth? (List them)
2. What books, audios, and seminars can help me find and achieve my purpose on earth? (List them)
3. What does God's word say about my Purpose/assignment? (List them)
4. What Activities should I do that can help me live a purpose-driven life? (List them)

Health Side

What is the way forward?

1. What is a scriptural prescription for good health and long life? (List them)

2. What is the right food, vitamins, or supplement to take? (List them)?

3. How do I improve in my health side? (List them)
4. what books, audios, and seminars can help me have a healthy lifestyle? (List them)
5. What does God's word say about my Health? (List them)
6. What activities should I do that can help me live Healthy life? (List them)

Finance Side
What is the way forward?

1. How do I improve my finance? (State it)
2. What is God's word toward my finance? (List them)
3. How do I get consistent cash flow that will make me retire early in life? (List them)
4. What is one change I could make today that would improve my finances? (List them)
5. How did I change and form lasting financial habits? (List them)
6. What books, audios, seminars, and investments can help build my finance? (List them)
7. What Activities should I engage in to build my finance? (List them)

YEARLY PLANS	MONTH	WEEK	WEEKLY PLAN	HOW	MEDIA NEEDED
	DATE	FIRST WEEK			
		SECO ND WEEK			
		THIRD WEEK			
		FOUR TH WEEK			
	DATE	FIRST WEEK			
		SECO ND WEEK			
		THIRD WEEK			

		FOUR TH WEEK			
	DATE	FIRST WEEK			
		SECO ND WEEK			
		THIRD WEEK			
		FOUR TH WEEK			
	DATE	FIRST WEEK			
		SECO ND WEEK			
		THIRD WEEK			

		FOUR TH WEEK			
	DATE	FIRST WEEK			
		SECO ND WEEK			
		THIRD WEEK			
		FOUR TH WEEK			
	DATE	FIRST WEEK			
		SECO ND WEEK			
		THIRD WEEK			

		FOUR TH WEEK			

Having done all this, be determined, be disciplined, be consistent, go back subsequently, review and check your progress and how far you have gone.

Be the best of yourself.

ABOUT EPISTLE

Realities of life with kingdom solutions

Epistle can be categorized into 3 M's (Ministry, Message, Me)

1. **Epistle as a Ministry (The rise of a Generation)**

Epistle- the rise of a generation is a ministry aimed at raising young people to **Know** God, **Grow** in the knowledge of God and **Influence** their world positively for God. It is a movement to rise and raise young armies/representatives for God.

2. **Epistle as a Message (Books)**

Epistle is a letter written/spoken to the church/believers/the body of Christ concerning the things which be, and addressing issues amongst the body (the church) as becoming saint, as seen from Apostle Paul. The original founder of Epistles (Peace be unto you Sir) a laborer and prisoner of our Lord Jesus Christ

These epistles by Precious James are basically Realities of life (things happening in our daily life) with kingdom solutions. They come in short stories, and speeches, but are edifying with principles of the kingdom

3. **Epistle as Me (A person)**

I am an Epistle KNOWN and READ by all men; YOU are an

Epistle- the message, the letter that we read (2 Cor. 3:2)

An epistle is an example (Pattern/Model/Template) of the believers (1 Timothy 4:12b)

Be An Epistle Today!!!

CHECK OUT OTHER LIFE-CHANGING EPISTLES BY PRECIOUS JAMES!!!

- **THE THINGS AROUND OUR NECK**
- **SECOND CHANCE**
- **COME BACK DEMAS**
- **WASTED YEARS OF YESTER-YEARS**
- **WHAT LIFE STOLE FROM ME**
- **TEARS OF WISDOM**
- **BEAUTIES OF SINGLE-HOOD**
- **UNFAIR ADVANTAGE**
- **FATHERS OF THE-MORROW**
- **THE PURSUIT OF YOUR STAR**
- **HELP US!!! THE MINISTRY OF THE AQUILIA'S**
- **NO EXCUSE**
- **WHAT NEXT? NOW THAT I AM SAVED**
- **MY HEART BEATS FOR YOU**
- **MY SEXUAL ADDICTION**

AND LOTS MORE...

OTHER BOOKS BY THE SAME AUTHOR

Becoming books are entrepreneurship books by Precious James aimed to help you BECOME a person of value to yourself and then to the society at large, it fights laziness and gives you the positive push to start something and BECOME the best version of yourself.

1. **Bake the cake - A step-by-step guide/approach – Vol 1**
2. **Cake Decorating – Buttercream techniques - Vol 2**
3. **Advance cake decorating with fondant - Vol 3**
4. **Whipped Cream Decorating – Stable whipped cream recipe - Vol 4**
5. **How to make yummy Meat-pie – Vol 5**
6. **How to make small chops (samosa, spring roll, Puff-puff, peppered meat/chicken) – Vol 6**
7. **How to make Yummy Chin-Chin – Vol 7**
8. **How to make homemade shawarma – Vol 8**
9. **How to make Peanut Burger – EASY STEPS – Vol 9**
10. **How to make Sausage Roll – Vol 10**
11. **How to make Eggroll and Buns – Vol 11**
12. **How to make Yummy Bread – Vol 12**
13. **How to make yummy Doughnut (Ring and Pillow Doughnuts) – Vol 13**

and lots more

FOR CONTACT INFORMATION

YouTube: Epistle- The rise of a Generation

Facebook: Epistle

Instagram: Epistle worldwide

Call/WhatsApp: +2348108826904

ABOUT THE AUTHOR

PRECIOUS JAMES is a passionate lover of God, a graduate of mechanical engineering from the University of Port-Harcourt, Nigeria.

She is a Writer, Teacher of God's word, and Entrepreneur, she has her Cake and Perfume line and she is the founder of the ministry "Epistle-The rise of a Generation" she is passionate about raising a God-driving, influential, and mighty Generation

She writes Epistles, these are true life realities with kingdom solutions, divinely inspired by the holy spirit of God, so we can be an Epistle (Model, Pattern, Template) of the believers (1 Timothy 4:12b)

Connect with her on Facebook: precious James and Instagram: _preciousjames_

www.ingramcontent.com/pod-product-compliance
Lightning Source LLC
LaVergne TN
LVHW020531160826
845677LV00015B/4000